"William's jokes are [...] recommend this book [...] in smiling, enjoys laug[...] ing. It's a must in your book collection!"

Justin, YouTube host and epic adventurer of JStu

"When I read this book, I feel like I'm the egg that's getting cracked up! I think William Daniel is hilarious, and I'm so glad that now the world will know too."

Braddock Musilli

"I always knew my friend William was funny, but I didn't know he was THIS funny! This book is a treasure trove of great jokes that will keep you and your friends laughing all day long!"

Sam Brightwell

"Knock knock. Who's laughing . . . we are! This book will make you laugh and help you be a funnier person to all those around you with so many unique and clever jokes to keep you smiling all day."

William Cassidy

"I loved reading all of the jokes in this book! The variety of subjects covered made them very entertaining. They're super easy to understand and are directed toward younger audiences, making them great for kids."

Aubrey Pantusa

"I love the variety of jokes! This collection of jokes really reflects Will's sense of humor."

Lauren Pantusa

"So funny it will make you cry!"

Hays Marks

"This book is laugh-out-loud hilarious!"

William Marks

"Every single joke is a completely original one I had never heard before. Whoever is looking at these words right now should undoubtedly buy this book. You and your family will laugh over and over at all these jokes no matter how many times you've read them before."

Celia Rae

"So creative and funny! A great way to bring smiles to people's faces!"

Ella Goudie

"I found William's jokes incredibly funny, and I enjoyed sharing them with my friends and family!"

Skye Goudie

YOU'RE
JOKING ME

BOOK 1

BURST OUT LAUGHING

YOU'RE JOKING ME

JOKES FOR KIDS BY A KID

WILLIAM DANIEL

SPIRE

Published by Revell
a division of Baker Publishing Group
PO Box 6287, Grand Rapids, MI 49516-6287
www.revellbooks.com

Printed in the United States of America

Library of Congress Cataloging-in-Publication Data
Names: Daniel, William, 2009– author.
Title: You're joking me : jokes for kids by a kid / William Daniel.
Other titles: You are joking me
Description: Grand Rapids, MI : Revell, a division of Baker Publishing Group, 2022. | Series: Burst out laughing ; 1 | Audience: Ages 6–8 Audience: Grades 2–3
Identifiers: LCCN 2022006245 | ISBN 9780800741341 (trade paperback) | ISBN 9781493438969 (ebook)
Subjects: LCSH: Wit and humor, Juvenile. | CYAC: Wit and humor. | Jokes. | LCGFT: Humor.
Classification: LCC PN6166 .D36 2022 | DDC 818/.602—dc23/eng/20220310
LC record available at https://lccn.loc.gov/2022006245

The author is represented by the literary agency of The Blythe Daniel Agency, Inc.

Baker Publishing Group publications use paper produced from sustainable forestry practices and post-consumer waste whenever possible.

22 23 24 25 26 27 28   7 6 5 4 3 2 1

To my grandfather
JAMES McINTOSH
for passing on his humor to me
and my father
ART DANIEL
who keeps me laughing.

Q: How do you find out how much fruit was on each tree in the beginning of creation?

A: You Adam up.

Q: What is a golfer's favorite drink?

A: Tee.

Q: What happens when a pony sings?

A: He gets a little hoarse.

Q: **What happens when snowmen get nervous?**

A: They get cold feet.

Q: **What did the pet store employee say to the customer when he couldn't speak clearly?**

A: "Cat got your tongue?"

Q: **Why did the guy stand on a microwaved calendar?**

A: He wanted to be on a hot date.

Q: **What do dinosaurs mine with?**

A: Dino-mite.

Q: **What is a pig's best talent?**

A: Bakin'.

Q: **What insect is the warmest?**

A: A yellow jacket.

Q: **What piece of cloth is the sleepiest?**

A: A napkin.

Q: **What did the announcer say about the race against two electricians?**

A: "It was down to the wire."

Q: **What did the cat say when he fell into the river?**

A: "Are you kitten me?"

Q: **What type of wood do people make shoes out of?**

A: Sandalwood.

Q: **What did the candy store owner have when he was sad?**

A: He had chocolatiers.

Q: What is a sock's favorite sport?

A: Soccer.

Q: What is the fattest fruit?

A: A plumpkin.

Q: What did one car say to the other car?

A: "You're driving me crazy."

Q: How do you know if a fashion model is your enemy?

A: If they pose a threat.

Q: **Why was Billie's garden so short?**

A: Because it was a yard.

Q: **Why did the guy do a marathon to the White House?**

A: He was running for president.

Q: **How did the bodiless man win the race?**

A: He was a head.

Q: **What did the lightning bolt say to the tornado?**

A: "You stole my thunder."

Q: **What is the best tool to practice with?**

A: A drill.

Q: **What did the candy store owner say to the customer?**

A: "It's a pretty sweet deal."

Q: **Why was the baker so rich?**

A: He had lots of dough.

Q: **Which composer is used for opening doors?**

A: Handel.

Q: **Why do trash can movies earn a lot of money?**

A: They get a high grossing.

Q: **Why did no one laugh at the boxer's joke?**

A: He didn't have a good punch line.

Q: **What did one glue bottle say to another glue bottle when they were entering the maze?**

A: "Let's stick together."

Q: Who are the best friends in technology?

A: The earbuds.

Q: Why did the golfer go to the laundromat?

A: She wanted to get a new iron.

Q: What is a chef's favorite motorcycle?

A: A chopper.

Q: What is a dog's favorite type of story?

A: A fairy tail.

Q: **What happened when the guy threw his bowl of cereal into the lake?**

A: He skipped breakfast.

Knock knock.

Who's there?

Yeah.

Yeah who?

Why are you so excited, is it your birthday?

Knock knock.

Who's there?

Dusty.

Dusty who?

Dusty have a minute to help me?

Q: What do pickles put in their gardens?

A: Daffodills.

Q: What is a scientist's favorite breed of dog?

A: A labrador.

Q: Where do sharks go on vacation?

A: Finland.

Q: What type of vegetable do chickens eat?

A: Eggplant.

Q: **What happened when the guy messed with time?**

A: He got clocked.

Q: **What type of candy do auto mechanics eat?**

A: Caramel.

Knock knock.

Who's there?

Howard.

Howard who?

Howard you doing today?

Knock knock.

Who's there?

Linda.

Linda who?

Will you Linda hand?

Knock knock.

Who's there?

Can.

Can who?

Can you reach my jacket from there?

Q: What happens when a musician gets in trouble?

A: There will B major consequences.

Knock knock.

Who's there?

Marble.

Marble who?

It's so marblous to see you.

Q: **How do you make a chair rock?**

A: You give it a guitar.

Q: **What do cakes say to each other while playing baseball?**

A: "Batter up!"

Q: Why was the plant so big?

A: It had a growth sprout.

Q: What happened when the guy tripped over the guitar?

A: It ended on a low note.

Knock knock.

Who's there?

Janeen.

Janeen who?

Janeen a ride home?

Knock knock.

Who's there?

Phillip.

Phillip who?

I'm here to Phillip your car.

Knock knock.

Who's there?

Can.

Can who?

Can you help me out the door?

Knock knock.

Who's there?

Art.

Art who?

Art you the one who came by my house?

Knock knock.

Who's there?

Kazoo.

Kazoo who?

More candy, kazoo's counting!

Knock knock.

Who's there?

Igloo.

Igloo who?

Igloo-ed on without my help.

Q: **Why did the grizzly say stop to the annoying raccoon?**

A: He couldn't bear it.

Q: **Why didn't the pair of scissors finish its project?**

A: Its time got cut short.

Q: **Why are race car drivers so hungry?**

A: They live the fast life.

Q: **What do grocery store baggers do when they play football?**

A: Sack people.

Q: **Why did the king not like the clouds moving on?**

A: It took away his reign.

Q: **What is a hunter's favorite flavor of ice cream?**

A: Moose tracks.

Q: **Why was the salsa maker mad?**

A: He had a chip on his shoulder.

Q: **What did the runner say to the pig during the race?**

A: "I'll meat you ahead."

Q: **What happened when the guy hit the golf ball into the lake?**

A: He sank a putt.

Q: **Why was the mushroom so popular?**

A: He was a fungi!

Q: **What do bakers put in their gardens?**

A: Flours.

Q: **What kind of cheese do people live in?**

A: Cottage cheese.

Q: **Where do spiders shop?**

A: On the web.

Q: **What do you do at the end of a speech about presents?**

A: You wrap it up.

Knock knock.

Who's there?

Water.

Water who?

Water you eating for dinner?

Q: What did the corn say when it lost the game?

A: "Ah, shucks."

Q: How do you transport a foot?

A: With a toe truck!

Q: Why was One dating Two?

A: Because he was single.

Q: Why did the man trip on the carpet?

A: It was rugged.

Q: Why was the TV lost?

A: It was in a remote area.

Q: What kind of plane cleans?

A: Crop dusters.

Q: What do you call a sock's best friend?

A: Its sole mate!

Q: Why was the pencil bored?

A: It felt dull.

Q: How did the hammerhead shark do on the test?

A: He nailed it.

Q: What is a boat's favorite game?

A: Yacht-zee.

Q: **What is an annoying person's favorite game?**

A: Poke-er.

Q: **Why did the lump of dough win the race?**

A: It was on a roll.

Q: **What did the underpants company do today?**

A: They had a brief meeting.

Q: Why did someone scream when the dresser came out of the bathroom?

A: It forgot to pull up its drawers.

Q: Why is deer feed so cheap?

A: It's only worth a buck.

Knock knock?

Who's there?

Snow.

Snow who?

There's snow way I'm going out in the cold.

Knock knock.

Who's there?

Donut.

Donut who?

I donut want to burn the cake.

Q: Which painting is the most bored?

A: The Moan-alisa.

Q: What do coffee sellers do in jail?

A: They take mug shots.

Q: Why should you have five quarters instead of five pennies?

A: It makes more cents.

Q: Where are expensive breath refreshments made?

A: The mint.

Q: What do cats use when baking?

A: A whisk-er.

Q: Want to hear a joke about a farmer?

A: Never mind, it's too corny.

Q: What kind of hardware do chipmunks eat?

A: Nuts.

Q: Have you heard of the new plane/car hybrid?

A: It's plane crazy!

Q: Why was the guitarist wet when he was playing with the band?

A: He was in the sync.

Q: What do vegetables use when cooking?

A: A beet-er.

Knock knock?

Who's there?

Clothes.

Clothes who?

Aren't you going to clothes the door?

Q: Why can't dogs finish movies?

A: They always paws it.

Knock knock.

Who's there?

Justin.

Justin who?

You're Justin time for dinner.

Q: Why was the golfer so thirsty?

A: He was par-ched.

Q: What do baseball players eat on?

A: Base plates.

Q: What does a young guy do when his lips hurt?

A: He puts on chaps-stick.

Q: Did you hear about the argument between the elevator and the building?

A: It escalated quickly!

Knock knock.

Who's there?

Needle.

Needle who?

Needle little push?

Knock knock.

Who's there?

Gopher.

Gopher who?

Gopher me to the grocery store?

Q: Why is a banker so healthy?

A: He has a clean bill of health!

Q: Why couldn't anybody see the spider's face on the call?

A: She forgot to turn on her webcam.

Q: **Why did the portrait get arrested?**

A: It got framed.

Q: **Why do people take water from baseball players?**

A: Because some of them are pitchers.

Q: **What do you call a lazy french fry?**

A: A couch potato.

Q: **Why did the guy choose the broken plate at the buffet?**

A: Somebody told him to fix a plate.

Knock knock.

Who's there?

Russian.

Russian who?

Russian me to school again?

Q: **What did the llama say to the camel when she was going on vacation?**

A: "Alpaca toothbrush."

Q: **Who cleans the dogs for a wedding?**

A: The groom.

Q: Why was the baker running around the kitchen?

A: He was going stir crazy.

Q: What happened when the skeleton got scared?

A: He jumped out of his skin.

Q: What do bodybuilders eat at seafood restaurants?

A: Muscles.

Q: How do you know if a light bulb is going to a good school?

A: Its future is bright.

Q: What kind of electronic device do pharmacists make?

A: A tablet.

Q: What do shoe designers do when they turn on their computers?

A: They let it boot up.

Knock knock.

Who's there?

Raisin.

Raisin who?

Jesus has raisin from the dead!

Q: What kind of bugs do you find in clocks?

A: Ticks.

Q: What fruit is used to cut?

A: A pear of scissors.

Q: What birds are used at construction sites?

A: Cranes.

Q: What can you find in a pig's toolbox?

A: A ham-mer.

Q: What do surfers put their drinks on?

A: Coasters.

Q: Why did the grocery store employee get in trouble?

A: She spilled the beans in front of a customer.

Q: What do trees do when signing into an account?

A: They log in.

Q: Why should you never do a staring contest with stairs?

A: They stairwell.

Q: How do you find stuff in an atlas?

A: You look in the table of continents.

Q: Why is it hard to make a joke to a tree?

A: It's a real stickler about things.

Q: What do baby chickens like to buy at stores?

A: Cheep cheep stuff.

Knock knock.

Who's there?

Yolk.

Yolk who?

Even though I fell, I'm yolk-ay.

Q: **What rank is a piece of popcorn in the army?**

A: A colonel.

Q: **How do you measure coins?**

A: With cent-imeters.

Q: **What animal doesn't play fair?**

A: A cheetah.

Q: **Why could the soil afford so much?**

A: It was rich.

Q: **What will you hear if a farmer does the weather forecast?**

A: On Tuesday it will be parsley cloudy.

Q: **Why is it hard to wash windows?**

A: Because they are a pane.

Q: What do you drink when you have a cold?

A: Cough-ee.

Q: Where do you weigh a dog?

A: At the pound.

Q: What kind of dessert does the alphabet like?

A: Brown-E's.

Q: Which instrument do ears play?

A: The eardrum.

Q: What kind of corn gives people endurance?

A: Grits.

Q: Why couldn't the tree solve the problem?

A: He was stumped.

Q: What did the tailor say when her client refused to pay?

A: "Sew it seams."

Q: What stationery tool do you use to keep animals in one area?

A: A pen.

Q: What do you call a recovering tree?

A: A syc-no-more.

Q: What kind of metal do thieves use?

A: Steel.

Q: What is a computer's favorite snack?

A: Chips.

Q: How do dogs go see the world?

A: They em-bark on journeys.

Q: What is a cool trampoline trick?

A: Handsprings.

Q: What did the duck say after surgery?

A: "I'll pay for the bill."

Q: What do dog owners wear under their pants?

A: Boxers.

Q: **Where do you go when your stomach is on trial?**

A: The food court.

Q: **Where do presidents store their dishes?**

A: In cabinets.

Q: **How do you make a pig's breath fresher?**

A: You use different pig-mints.

Q: **How come golfers never crash their golf carts?**

A: They're good drivers.

Q: **How do golfers play games?**

A: The fairway.

Q: **Why did the cow preach at church?**

A: He was the pasture of the church.

Q: **Why didn't the boy eat during dinner?**

A: He said he had a lot of homework on his plate.

Q: **What kind of animal is used for technology?**

A: A mouse.

Q: **What happened to the tourist on his vacation?**

A: He tripped.

Q: **Where does the hunter file his taxes?**

A: At the taxidermy.

Q: **What did the clock say to the wall?**

A: "Watch this."

Q: How did the boy feel about the mosquitoes?

A: He was itching for them to leave.

Knock knock.

Who's there?

Ice cream.

Ice cream who?

Ice cream if you don't let me in.

Q: What does a penny smell like?

A: I don't know, but it's a mighty cent.

Q: **How did the battery win the race?**

A: He got a jump start.

Knock knock.

Who's there?

Canoe.

Canoe who?

Canoe take out the trash?

Q: **Where do ants go on vacation?**

A: Antarctica.

Q: Why was the boy's homework missing?

A: He claimed it was a breeze.

Q: How bad is it to fix a roof?

A: The shingle worst thing.

Q: What do you say when a bird comes flying at your face?

A: "Duck!"

Q: Why can you never trust grass?

A: 'Cause it always stalks you.

Q: **How do you weigh a fish?**

A: With scales.

Q: **What do sharks listen to?**

A: Killer tunes.

Q: **Why did the boy put a speaker on his toast?**

A: He had some jams playing.

Q: **What did the bee say to his girlfriend?**

A: "Honey, won't you bee mine?"

Q: How do you find your favorite breakfast snack?

A: You look up its cereal number.

Q: What did the horse say when she disapproved of something?

A: "Nay."

Knock knock.

Who's there?

Butternut squash.

Butternut squash who?

You butternut squash my plants.

Q: Why was the US citizen happy?

A: He was in a good state.

Knock knock.

Who's there?

Wire.

Wire who?

Wire you waiting in that line?

Q: What's a landscaper's favorite sport?

A: Fencing.

Q: What did one computer manufacturer say to the other when they were bargaining?

A: "You make a hard drive!"

Q: Which country is a marine animal?

A: Wales.

Q: How do you get across a library in one second?

A: You book it.

Q: What do mountains wear when the temperature drops?

A: Snowcaps.

Q: What did the trumpet say when it scared the guitar?

A: "Do not fret."

Q: Which piece of hardware is used for cleaning clothes?

A: Washers.

Q: How do lawyers like their mattresses?

A: Firm.

Q: **What is the best thing about a job designing barns?**

A: It's stable.

Knock knock.

Who's there?

Berry.

Berry who?

It was berry nice of you to give me a gift.

Q: **How did the baseball player eat dinner?**

A: He stepped up to the plate.

Q: How does a computer eat?

A: In small bytes.

Q: What did the sloth say to his wife?

A: "I love you slow much."

Q: What is the best time to finish eating?

A: Ate o'clock.

Q: Which type of haircut do bees get?

A: A buzz cut.

Q: Why didn't the car listen to the wheel?

A: Because it spoke too much.

Q: Why did the kid hold up a piece of meat during the game?

A: Somebody told him to raise the steaks.

Q: What do swimmers play in their free time?

A: Pool.

Q: How does Mother Nature light up her home?

A: With bulbs.

Q: Why was the pig mad at his computer?

A: He had spam mail.

Q: What did the pirate say to his doctor when he was asked what hurts?

A: "Eye, Matey."

Q: **Which family member is the most beloved in the insect family?**

A: The aunt.

Q: **What time do sailors go shopping?**

A: When there's a big sail.

Q: **What kind of pig drills through rock?**

A: A boar.

Q: **What happened to the boy when he took a nap?**

A: He got cot in the sheets.

Q: How do you know if a grape is victorious?

A: If it concord everything.

Q: What happened to the dill when he got stuck?

A: He was in a pickle.

Q: What do you say when your doctor is allergic to apples?

A: "An apple a day keeps the doctor away!"

Q: Which metal is used as law enforcement?

A: Cop-per.

Q: How did the baseball player do on his test?

A: He knocked it out of the park.

Q: Why does paper never move?

A: It's always stationery.

Q: What do army soldiers wear in the summer?

A: Tank tops.

Q: What did the astronaut say when he was happy?

A: "I'm on top of the world!"

Q: Why was the whale sad?

A: He was feeling blue.

Q: Why did the chair thief get away with everything?

A: Everybody told him to take a seat.

Q: What did the coin need when his clothes got messy?

A: A change.

*I couldn't think of what
taste buds were called;
it was on the tip of my tongue.*

Q: **How come the pickle didn't attend
the school dance?**

A: He didn't relish the idea.

Q: **What do you get when you cross a
rich man and a lighter?**

A: Somebody with money to burn.

Knock knock.

Who's there?

Summer.

Summer who?

Can you get me summer water?

Q: What kind of rock is used for lawsuits?

A: Quartz.

Q: What do car speakers like to watch in their free time?

A: Car-tunes.

Q: What did the shoe repairman say to the fly?

A: "Shoe!"

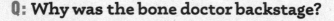

Q: Why was the bone doctor backstage?

A: He was a cast member.

Q: What did the astronaut say to the other astronaut when he was upset?

A: "You better comet down."

Q: How could you tell that the pharmacist was annoying?

A: He was being a pill.

Q: **What do hunters do on Easter?**

A: They go egg hunting.

Q: **What happens when you eat too much?**

A: You get chewed out.

Q: **What did the golfer say when someone asked him if he liked the sport?**

A: "Of course I do!"

Q: **Why don't fruit go skydiving?**

A: They plum-met.

Q: Why didn't the turkey finish his dinner?

A: He was stuffed.

Q: Why don't bulls work in restaurants?

A: Because they overcharge people.

Q: Which nut is used for making houses?

A: Wall-nuts.

Q: What happened to the clothing designer in the boxing match?

A: He got socked.

Q: What did the plate say to the knife?

A: "You're a cut up."

Q: What did the car say to the truck after someone put beans in the fuel tank?

A: "I've got gas."

Q: What is a potato's favorite game?

A: Two truths and a fry.

Q: Why was the piece of bread in a play?

A: Because he had a roll.

Q: What did the gnat want when his boss was mean to him?

A: He wanted to flea the place.

Q: How did the miner do at the party?

A: He had a blast.

Q: Why did medieval people rarely see the sun?

A: Because it was the dark ages and there were many knights.

Q: Why did the guy glue the blueprint to himself?

A: He wanted to stick to his plan.

Q: What does an elephant use for luggage?

A: A trunk.

Q: What did the zookeeper do about the new animal?

A: He announced the elephant in the room.

Q: What time does a farmer wake up?

A: Quarter till seven.

Q: What did the vegetables say before they started eating?

A: "Lettuce pray."

Q: What did the burrito say about the quesadilla?

A: "He sure does taco lot about sauces!"

Q: Can the artist paint mountains?

A: He can easel-ly do it.

Q: **What was the baker doing with the ingredients?**

A: He was pudding them in the bowl.

Q: **What did the bee use to fix his hair?**

A: A honeycomb.

Q: **What happens when you give an electrician coffee?**

A: He becomes wired.

Q: **What type of animal likes vegetables?**

A: A unicorn.

Q: Which tool in a workshop government is second in command?

A: The vise president.

Knock knock.

Who's there?

Olive.

Olive who?

Olive you guys come here.

Q: What did the farmer use to eat his breakfast?

A: A pitchfork.

Q: What kind of mattress remembers things?

A: Memory foam.

Q: What did the nucleus use to call the mitochondria?

A: A cell phone.

Q: What kind of stories do giraffes like to listen to?

A: Tall tales!

Q: **What did the peanut say to the walnut?**

A: "I want nut-tin to do with this."

Q: **What did the fireman say when he saw a burning building?**

A: "Holy smokes!"

Knock knock.

Who's there?

Grant.

Grant who?

I will grant you five bucks.

Q: Which city in Italy makes people lost?

A: Rome.

Q: Did you hear about the meteor?

A: It impacted our studies.

Q: What do you get when you cross a sour candy and a boxer?

A: Something that packs a punch.

Q: What did the boxer say to the avacado?

A: "I'ma guac your socks off!"

*I don't really like learning about
the human skin,
but it is growing on me.*

Q: **What is a trampoline's favorite
season?**

A: Spring.

Q: **What is a lightning bolt's favorite
superhero?**

A: The Flash!

Knock knock.

Who's there?

Batter.

Batter who?

You'd batter open the door!

Q: What kind of weapon do felines use?

A: Cat-a-pults.

Q: What did the theme park employee experience when he was fired?

A: A roller coaster of emotions.

I couldn't figure out how my camera worked and then it clicked.

I tried making an airplane, but it never took off.

Q: **How did the gardener help make the cake?**

A: She was the sprinkler.

Q: **What did the farmer say when he was finishing his vacation?**

A: "I can't wheat to go home."

Q: What's a farmer's favorite game?

A: Cornhole.

Q: What kind of footwear makes things slick?

A: Slippers.

Q: What do you call twelve twirling muffins?

A: A-bun-dance.

Q: What do you call it when you finally turn on your car's transmission?

A: Something that came in a clutch.

Q: **Why did the football player tap the ground?**

A: He wanted to get a touchdown.

Q: **What do you get when you cross a bean and a watermelon?**

A: The fruit that makes you toot!

Q: **What does a flooring installer do when he exercises?**

A: Planks.

Q: What do you call an alpaca that is part of the senate?

A: A law-ma.

Q: Why did the criminal climb on the roof of the courthouse?

A: He wanted to be above the law.

Q: What did the barber say to his mad companion?

A: "You need to comb down."

Q: What did the guy do when he saw a cow in the road?

A: He steered out of the way.

Q: What did the fork say to the knife?

A: "You look sharp!"

Q: What happened when the spool of thread put too many things on his calendar?

A: He got wound up.

Q: What do you call a meeting between an iron and an ironing board?

A: A press conference.

Q: What do you call a female deer in a bakery?

A: A doe.

Q: What do you call a T. rex with wings?

A: A dino-soar.

Q: Where does the electrician go shopping?

A: The outlet mall.

Q: Did you hear about the crashed news van?

A: It was breaking news.

Q: Where did the farmer get his medicine?

A: The farm-acy.

Q: What piece of clothing is the laziest?

A: Slacks.

Q: Did you hear about the geometry malfunction?

A: The aftermath was surprising.

Q: **Why did no one laugh at the tumbleweed's joke?**

A: He had a dry sense of humor.

Q: **Why didn't the guy make a lot of rope?**

A: His time got cut short.

Q: **Why was the tumbleweed sad?**

A: He was down in the dust.

Q: **What is a roll's favorite sport?**

A: Biscuit ball.

Q: What is the slipperiest country?

A: Greece.

Q: What did the farmer say when he dropped his crops?

A: "Hoe no!"

Q: What did the house wear to the wedding?

A: Ad-dress.

I tried making some camera jokes, but it was all just a blur.

Q: **What did the chef say when he wanted something done fast?**

A: "Chop, chop!"

Q: **How do you set up a table for a clothing designer?**

A: In an orderly fashion.

I really liked climbing mountains, but it went downhill from there.

Q: **What do you call a zoo escape?**

A: A panda-monium!

Q: **What did the cow think about the party?**

A: He was udderly surprised.

Q: **What do you call a deer fresh out of the shower?**

A: Buck naked.

Q: **What did the guy eat for lunch when he had a cold?**

A: Mac and sneeze.

Q: **When does a baseball player do yoga?**

A: When he is on the home stretch.

Q: What do you call a bird in shining armor?

A: A knight owl.

Q: What did the deer eat for breakfast?

A: Doe-nuts.

Q: How does a tree make a New Year's resolution?

A: He turns a new leaf.

Q: What do you call someone who steals circles?

A: A pi-rate.

Q: **Why couldn't the window see?**

A: He had blind-ers.

Q: **How did the fisherman catch the fish?**

A: He waded awhile.

Q: **Where do bad rainbows go?**

A: To prism with a light sentence.

Q: **What did the American president say to the governor?**

A: "State your claim."

Q: Where do llamas go skiing?

A: In the Alp-acas.

Q: What do you call a flaming muffin?

A: A hot cake.

Q: Want to hear a joke about the wind?

A: Never mind, it's a blow.

Q: What did the guy think when his ugly lamp was stolen?

A: He was de-lighted.

Q: Which muscle is the strongest in a cow?

A: The calf.

Q: How could you tell the toilet was sick?

A: He was flushed.

Q: How did the thermometer get his job?

A: He had a good degree from college.

Q: What did the scientist use to keep her breath fresh?

A: Experi-mints.

Q: What do you call a computer's parent?

A: Motherboard.

The man's wife had a baby.
A-parent-ly he's a father now!

Q: When can you know how much a cake weighs?

A: When it's a pound cake.

Q: **What is a potato at a football game?**

A: A spec-tator.

Q: **What did the crab say to his family at dinner?**

A: "Shell we eat?"

Q: **How did the man fall down the well?**

A: He couldn't see that well.

Q: **Why was the meteorologist not feeling well?**

A: He was under the weather.

Q: **Why were everybody's tires popping?**

A: There was a fork in the road.

Q: **What kind of mineral do you eat on?**

A: Table salt.

Q: **Why did the easy test get blown away?**

A: It was a breeze.

Q: **What did the farm animals say to the lamb who was leaving?**

A: "Sheep you later!"

Q: **What kind of musical band is in your shorts?**

A: The waist band.

Q: **Why did the guy eat the orange?**

A: It was a-peel-ing.

Q: **What happens when you have a runny nose?**

A: Well, it's snot my problem.

Q: **Why did no one like the cow?**

A: Because he was a bull-y.

Q: **How are cameras like windows?**

A: They both have shutters.

Q: **What do jazz players use to call each other?**

A: Saxo-phones.

Q: **Which country is the sweetest?**

A: Sweden.

Q: **What happens when a baker sleeps in?**

A: He is tart-y to work.

Q: What candy is used for seasoning soup?

A: Peppermint.

Q: What kind of plant hurts?

A: A face-plant.

Q: What kind of apples do you find on the beach?

A: Crab apples.

Q: What do elephants have in common with trees?

A: They both have trunks.

Q: **What is a carpet's favorite sport?**

A: Rug-by.

Q: **What do you say when a grape gets intense?**

A: "He's raisin the stakes!"

Q: **What do factory owners use to hold up their pants?**

A: Conveyer belts.

Q: **What do astronauts like to listen to?**

A: Nep-tunes.

Q: How does a train gather its thoughts?

A: It gets them back on track.

Q: Why did the guy name his dog Baguette?

A: Because it was pure bread.

Q: What did the lightning bolt do when it was mad?

A: It stormed out of the room.

Q: Where does a fly shop?

A: The flea market.

Q: What do you call an astronaut when he's hungry?

A: Ready for launch.

Q: What happened to the pumpkin when it got ran over?

A: It got squashed.

Q: What is the most unholy food?

A: Deviled eggs.

Q: What does a doctor use to keep his breath fresh?

A: Liga-mints.

Q: Which tool does a playing card use to dig up dirt?

A: A spade.

Word on the street is somebody spilled alphabet soup on the road.

Q: How does the moon cut his hair?

A: Eclipse it.

Q: What did the cow use to do construction?

A: Bull-dozers.

Q: What did one muffin say to the other muffin when they were in the oven?

A: "Is it just me, or is it hot in here?"

Q: What did the leopard say after lunch?

A: "That hit the spot."

Q: What did the obsidian say to the limestone?

A: "Don't take me for granite."

Q: Which animal is used for baseball?

A: The bat.

Q: **Where do fish sleep?**

A: In a riverbed.

Q: **What is a bird's favorite chip dip?**

A: Squawk-a-moly.

Q: **What is a tortilla chip's favorite dance?**

A: The salsa.

Q: **Why was the genie in the lamp upset?**

A: Somebody rubbed him the wrong way.

Q: **What is a crab's favorite part of pizza?**

A: The crust-acean.

Q: **What did the diver say during the investigation?**

A: "Let's get to the bottom of this."

*I was trying to find the sun
when it dawned on me.*

Q: **Why didn't the crab share?**

A: He was shellfish.

Q: What did the guy say when he threw a bottle of soda on the roof?

A: "Next one's on the house."

Q: How do dogs get around town?

A: In a wag-on.

Q: How did the pepper get on the soccer team?

A: He had a good kick.

Q: How much electricity does it take to power a house?

A: A watt.

Q: **Why were the sheets so happy when they got washed?**

A: They felt bed-der.

Q: **What is frustrating about working on a puzzle?**

A: The missing peace.

Q: **How do lawyers keep their breath fresh?**

A: With state-mints.

Q: How do you get from one end of a hardware store to the other?

A: You bolt.

Q: What do speakers study in math?

A: Volume.

Q: How did the wheel do its presentation?

A: It spoke.

Q: What happened when the bowler missed the last pin?

A: He was in de-spare.

Q: Why should you never do a competition with an elevator?

A: They always take it to the next level.

Q: Why didn't the snowman like the idea of melting?

A: He hadn't warmed up to it.

Q: Why should you never smash a light bulb?

A: It's not a bright idea.

Q: How did you get from Turkey to Pakistan?

A: Iran.

Q: How does a lumberjack get into a computer?

A: He logs in.

Q: Where do computers go to get a drink?

A: The space bar.

Q: What time does a tennis player wake up?

A: Ten-nish.

Q: What did God think when he needed somebody to build an ark?

A: I Noah guy.

Q: What did the vacuum say to himself when he fell?

A: "Suck it up!"

Q: What do you call a fat grape?

A: Plum-py.

Q: What do skeletons play in the band?

A: Trom-bones.

Q: **How come courthouses were well planned in biblical times?**

A: They had many judges.

Q: **Why did Moses like math?**

A: It has Numbers.

Q: **How do pest controllers work?**

A: On the fly.

Q: **What did the piano say to the flute?**

A: "Let's tune in."

Q: **What do you get when you have two dozen golden vegetables?**

A: Twenty-four carrot gold.

Q: **How did the baseball player do on his exam?**

A: He finished it right off the bat.

I didn't like climbing mountains, but I got over it.

Ceiling fans aren't my favorite thing, but they're up there.

A picture book went to prison.
It wasn't a long sentence.

Q: **Why was the raccoon sad?**

A: He was down in the dumps.

Q: **What does a car do when he eats too fast?**

A: He paces himself.

Q: **Why didn't the football player like circles?**

A: He was more of a lineman.

Q: **How fast does a tangled rope go on a ship?**

A: One hundred knots.

Q: **What do geologists eat off of?**

A: Tectonic plates.

Q: **What do you call a sick bucket?**

A: Pail.

Q: **How come One never wore size Two?**

A: It was two big.

Knock knock.

Who's there?

Oliver.

Oliver who?

Oliver flights were canceled.

Q: Why did chess never do anything active?

A: He was a bored game.

Knock knock.

Who's there?

Neil.

Neil who?

Neil a little closer and I'll tell you.

Knock knock.

Who's there?

Joey.

Joey who?

Jo-eat your donut yet?

Q: What type of clothing lives on in your family?

A: Genes.

Q: Why did the boy cut a big book into smaller pieces?

A: He made a long story short.

Knock knock.

Who's there?

Alaska.

Alaska who?

Alaska you once.

Q: What do you call a cute panel with hinges?

A: A-door-able.

Q: What did the sea lion do when he found a crack in his bucket?

A: He sealed it up.

Q: What did the rope say to the pulley when he was being critical?

A: "Cut me some slack!"

Q: What is the oldest cheese?

A: Aged cheddar.

Q: Why didn't the girl want her best friend to play sports with her?

A: She didn't want to socc-er.

Q: Why didn't the astronaut bring back any moon rock?

A: There wasn't any space for it.

Q: Why do dogs have so many friends?

A: They're part of a woof pack.

Knock knock.

Who's there?

Turnip.

Turnip who?

Turnip the heat; I'm freezing!

Q: Want to hear a joke about an unmailed letter?

A: Never mind, it's still coming to me.

Q: What is a lumberjack's favorite book in the Bible?

A: Acts.

Knock knock.

Who's there?

Anita.

Anita who?

Anita pencil for my test.

Knock knock.

Who's there?

Alyce.

Alyce who?

Alyce you didn't get stuck out in the cold.

Knock knock.

Who's there?

Conya.

Conya who?

Conya open the door?

Knock knock.

Who's there?

Dee-jay.

Dee-jay who?

Dee-jay win the game?

Q: What is the best road for a gymnast?

A: One with a good bend in it.

Q: What do you call an alligator who steals things?

A: A crook-o-dile.

Q: What did the jeweler say to the customer buying a ring?

A: "It rocks."

Knock knock.

Who's there?

Lion.

Lion who?

Are you lion or telling the truth?

Q: What did the lumberjack say when he asked for a favor?

A: "Wood you be so kind?"

Q: What makes music in your hair?

A: A headband.

ACKNOWLEDGMENTS

I would like to thank Andrea Doering for believing in me and helping me through the stages of writing this book. Thank you for giving me this opportunity.

Thank you to Melanie Burkhardt and Sarah Traill for all that you are doing to market the book to ensure efficiency in sales.

I would also like to thank Erin Bartels for doing such a great job on creating great marketing copy.

Thank you to Sadina Grody Brott for thoroughly going through my book to look for things that could lessen the quality of the manuscript and for making sure that each of my words fit.

Thank you to my Grandad, James McIntosh, for giving me the humor that I have. Coming from a family that loves to laugh means a lot. And thank you to Nannie, Helen McIntosh, for listening to and laughing at all my jokes and sharing some of your own with me.

Thank you to my sisters Calyn and Maris for letting me try out jokes on you and for listening to me at the breakfast table.

I would like to thank my mom and agent Blythe Daniel for hooking me onto the idea of writing a book. Thank you for explaining to me how all of this works. I love you and I thank you for really helping me throughout the publishing process. And thank you to my dad, Art Daniel, for keeping me motivated.

I'm grateful to the entire team at Revell for allowing me to share my jokes with readers everywhere.

William Daniel is a sixth grader, a WWII enthusiast, and a competitive gymnast. He builds model airplanes and wants to be a pilot someday. He has an older sister, Maris, a twin sister, Calyn, and is younger by four minutes. As you can well imagine, he enjoys making people laugh, which he does for family, friends, and classmates. William lives in Colorado with his family and dog, Riley.

FOR MORE FUN AND HUMOR,
CONNECT WITH WILL

f @thewilliamdaniel

⊙ @thewilliamdanielauthor